First published in 2021 by Pauline Crampin
Copyright © Pauline Crampin, 2021.

The right of Pauline Crampin to be identified as the author
of this work has been asserted by her in accordance with the
Copyright, Designs and Patents Act. 1988.

All rights reserved. No part of this publication may be reproduced,
stored in a retrieval system, or transmitted in any form, or by any means
(electronic, mechanical, photocopying, recording or otherwise) without
prior written permission of the author.

Thank you to everyone who helped me in this project, especially
my Husband, who walked with me and Cinnia Bermingham.

ISBN 978-1-3999-0557-2

Printed by www.xlpress.co.uk
Scanned by www.artworksrepro.co.uk

For my seven Grandchildren.
They are our future.

COVID 19 Pandemic 2020

How it changed the world whilst the natural world flourished in the unpolluted sunny days of spring

18th February 2020

We arrived back from our holiday in Oman, Abu Dhabi and South Africa. We carefully negociated our way through Heathrow, and then the underground and train home. We were aware of the growing threat global travel was having on the spreading of the virus Covid 19.

However our lives continue as normal as there was no suggestion of self isolating. We kept a careful check on our health just in case the airport had given us more than we desired!

5th March

The FIRST death recorded from Covid 19 in uk

1

9th March

People were beginning to realise that the arrival of the virus that was raging in Italy and Europe would reach the UK soon. What preparation, was the government doing; investigating various scientific theories!

We prepared by John doing several thorough supermarket shops, but no stock piling, who wants 100's of loo rolls? I took the opportunity to play golf with people who had not been skiing in Italy. Bridge continued but we were beginning to think it was not safe to play — so much contact, of cards.

14th March
We decided to postpone Cawley Safari Supper — a wise move.

16th March
All over 70's, and vulnerable people told to self isolate
Bridge club closed for business.

22nd Mother's day,
Tom sent me a beautiful bouquet. The P.M. told all not to visit our mothers, many went to the beach

23rd March

All bridge and golf has been cancelled and this was the last day I ventured into Stamford, the first time wearing a mask. I had my ears syringed, I declined hearing test but promised to see doctor about abnormal right eardrum.

I bought vegetables from a market stall and refused his change. Visited Hambelton Bakery and butchers up Iron monger street and returned home feeling like a happy hunter.

My last shopping trip for weeks.

Dentist cancelled my appointment to fix wobbly implant, and the opticians the same for my glaucoma tests.

24th March

The sun shone and continued to for many weeks drying up the flooded field

Anna Crampin was tested positive to the covid virus, caught on a Morrocan expedition; was taken into isolation hospital. This is happening in Abu Dhabi where she is.

The prime minister announced the UK would go into lock down. However there was no holding back with nature 13

24th March

Daily walks with John begin for our regulation one hours exercise, outside. The sky was blue and the sun shone brightly. We were fortunate to enjoy many more weeks of warm sunny weather, which help keep spirits up.

So began my interest in observing nature in more detail than usual. Nature transformed itself more rapidly than usual because of the unseasonable amount of sun shine

Our first walk was to Shillingthorpe, starting from the car, across the fields being planted with spring wheat. A herd of deer loitered in the same field as the busy tractor. The ruin of the house, which had belonged to George III doctor was surrounded by primroses and daffodils and narcissus fluttering in the wind below the bare ash.

25th March.

The sun continues to shine and we see
our first cowslip on a sheltered grassy
field bank. We took the car then
walked on to Banthorp. The late blackthorn
blossom still a brilliant white in the
bare hedges.

26th March For the last time we took the
car to visit Rasselo for plant food and
primulas. The River Glen was running
fast and high after all the recent rain.

27th March All the schools closed, because
of the virus, with no indication when
they would return. Consequently all public
exams are suspended.

28th March The garden has dried up as have
the fields, in some cases like concrete !

29th March British summer Time begins, and
so does spring. very warm and sunny.

primrose

cowslip

5

29th March

Whilst walking along the local Carlby
fields we note how busy the farmers are.
What appeared to be cultivated fields
are being ploughed and planted up with
wheat. A few weeks ago the same fields
were sodden and flooded by the
riverside in Ryhall, For many weeks it
had rained ruining many crops leaving
the land unworkable.

APRIL

1st April This was to be the Opening of John's
first 2 man sculpture exhibition. It
was to be in Corby Glen memorial gallery
but was cancelled because of the
imposed social distancing policy.
Instead of working on his displays we
worked on the garden instead.

5th April It is Palm Sunday, I attended my first
'Zoom' church service, which was comforting.
First Brimstone Butterfly.

6th April We Recieved our first online grocery delivery from Morrisons, which was set up by Anna Crampin before she became too ill. We have been very worried at Anna's lack of progress and she is in very low spirits in isolation. This isolation continued for 28 days, the latter part being in overflow at the Hilton Hotel.

7th April We took advantage of the hot sunny weather by doing lots of gardening. We rearranged borders and made seed beds for vegetables by the composter. First orange tip butterfly

10th April John walked to the cross Roads and saw the first bluebells in nearby Spinney.

12th April EASTER after a video church service we walked to Dan's wood or Monks wood and were delighted to see more lush primroses and violets. To our surprise the far side was a carpet of bluebells bobbing in the dapple sun.

Monks wood bluebells

7

12th April On our return we celebrated Easter
with Suzanne and Alan, drinking
champagne and conversing over the
fence at a safe distant.
Anna remains in hospital and the
4 children only had little easter eggs.
the last in the Abu Dhabi shops. Tom's
family did better.
John saw our first swallow and I a house
martin fly over the garden.
13th April During our walk we noticed three
gates Removed on the Essendine Loop and
decided it was for health and safety in
this virus lock down. Discovered white
butterflies were the female orange tips!
I have never noticed how common and yet
So beautiful is the wild cherry in blossom.

swallows   house martins return   8

15th April

The cowslips on the grassverges have now
grown to their full height as they and grasses
competes for light. The hawthorn
hedgerows are no longer bare with
green leaf shoots everywhere.
The pair of blackbirds in the garden are
very busy feeding on all our lawns.
The fish are more numerous in the
west Glen and the surface feeders. possibly
trout are getting bigger. At the begining
of the journal we saw no fish in the river,
but as the water has warmed more food
must become available. It seems very early
for the oil seed rape fields to start
flowering. I am glad that there are far
fewer fields of bright yellow these days
as it can bring on the
asthma. The crab apple
blossom is beautiful now.

crab apple

Blackbirds

16th April

We walked to Braceborough woods to see the lush primroses and discovered a carpet of bluebells in the left side of the wood. The sun shone and the peacock butterflies danced, it was heaven!

It was the first time we noticed the oak leaves were unfurling well before the ash trees. We heard the first chiffchaff singing in the woods. I started my first zoom meeting of boys book group reading 'Secret seven' my favourite!

peacock butterfly 30mm

chiff-chaff

10

17th April

It rained in the night and continued the next day, thank goodness. We have gone from one of the wettest March's to the driest Aprils. Both garden and field crops needed this water and the West Glen stream rose in volume and spread under the bridge.

The hawthorn hedges are now budding and the crab apple blossom is peeping through:

The bare ash are now showing green spikes of leaves yet unfurled next to the dark purplish tiny male flowers

ash buds

ash flowers

a leaf unfurling

ash leaf

female ash keys

11

21st April
We parked the car on Pickworth Drift, and
walked to Ryhall Heath and Ryhall, "John
Clare's" country. The sun again shone brightly
bringing out all the early butterflies that
we had seen on previous walks, including
the female orangetip.
All the flowers seemed
to come out at once, the
white nettle being the
first and then the Redcampion
the tall cow parsley and   female orangetip
the creeping purple
bugle. It has been flowering
for weeks at a low level.

female orangetip

cow parsley

Red campion

Bugle

12

24th April

We walked along the West Glen which is at average flow after a very wet spring where it rose by around 4 feet flooding in places. During the dry April the water dropped becoming clear so we could easily see the sticklebacks and baby trout feeding on the surface. As the weeks go by the fish grow bigger and more numerous. As do the Rooks nesting in the spinney at Essendine, they are very noisy gregarious birds. Fortunately they are nesting high in the rather bare ash trees well away from the village. The hedges and trees are all greening up very rapidly in this warm sunny weather.

Essendine Spinney Rookery

13

25th April

On our way back from buying some farm eggs
we parked near Belmesthorpe Grange to take
a walk. We took the wrong path from
the beginning and headed towards Uffington
instead of Baunthorpe. It was another very hot
sunny day and we saw a pair of long tailed
tits feeding in the thick verdant hawthorn
hedge.

Long-tail tits

26th April on the Essendine Loop walk we
spotted our first blue butterfly. At first I
thought was a chalk Blue but on referring to the
book I found it was a holly blue feeding off tiny
Holly flowers.   It is very small and
                              delicate.

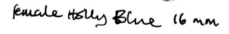

Female Holly Blue 16 mm

27th April

It was a cloudy morning and then 3 days of rain followed. consequently the fields and hedges turned from cinnamon colour to a huge range of greens. The West Glen flowed at high volume again and too murky to see the fish.

The grasses are starting to flower but I cannot identify them yet.

Bladder campion

Herb Robert

horsechestnut 15

1st May

After all the rain the weather has cleared
revealing acres upon acres of green fields, mostly
wheat or barley. I noticed that the oak tree
was flowering and the bank of cowslips was
going over losing its bright yellow colour.
The hedges are now a very thick barrier of
green hawthorn, now daintily decorated with
the white may flower.

oak blossom

May flower

3rd May After delivering a parcel to the
collection area we drove onto Caseirok
lane to walk in the park. The grass was
growing lush and tall with more flowers
than I can name. The oak was lime green
and some had feathery blossom, as
had the sycamore.
We heard the first cuckoo calling for his mate,
it calls on the wing and is hard to spot.
Tom's childrens produced a pop video by
their group 'Low Gravity' it was really great!!

16

4th May

My 71st birthday and the 7th week of lockdown.
During coffee break we watched a sparrow
hawk swooping down on the poor little
sparrows, fortunately they all escaped!

male sparrowhawk

English partridge
On our walk down the road we spotted our
English partridge couped down in the early
wheat field. When still he blended into the soil

6th May

Both the robin and blackbird are busy catching
worms for their young. We now have one
blackbirds nest in our bush, a robin in the front
hedge and a pigeon in the hawthorne tree on
the side. At a later date the collared
dove made a sparse nest
in the Rose arch.

collared doves

As we walked down the Road which is lined
with ash trees we noticed how different they
were. Some were in full leaf, others not at
all. Some with remains of dried dark flowers
but a few were laden with many thick
clusters of ash. Keys. Purple vetch was
just beginning to flower on the grass verges.

purple vetch

7th May

We walked along the side of the West Glen and noticed how very low the water was. The water was clear so we could see the small sticklebacks which were beginning to grow in just a few weeks. Earlier we had seen the surface feeding trout had grown, down by the road bridge. We sauntered through Essendine Spinney, the dappled sun shone through the ash, which were not fully out, illuminating the shoulder high swaying cow parsley.

I saw in the hedgrows the first flowers opening on both the Elder and guelder Rose.

guelder Rose

elder flower

8th May Bank Holiday for VE Day celebrations. Farriers Way held a socially distanced street tea party. It was fun. The blackbird who had always been very friendly hopped into our kitchen. I eventually released him through the window. Very hot again 23°C.

VE Day teaparty - Carlby

19

9th May

Another unseasonably hot day, reaching 25°C.
I peeped into the blackbirds nest to find 3
babies almost ready to leave.

10th May We walk down
the track to Marks wood
and saw a pied wagtail
on the path which was
covered in May blossom
like snow. Growing on the grass verge was
the first pink clover flowering alongside the
very first pale dog rose. Winter seems to have
returned with the temperature dropping 18°C
to 7°C in the daytime! It rained most of the

blackbirds nest

purple clover

day but the late sun shone
brightly on the early
buttercups on the wayside,
very cheering. Thank goodness
for the beauty of nature to
cheers us up in these difficult
times.

buttercup   20

11th May
The goveraments slogan 'stay at home has now
changed to stay alert which has led to
initial confusion but people are being encourage
to return to work. We are now allowed to exercise
outside twice a day and drive any distance to
other areas for recreation. When the virus spike
occures, which is inevitable in about 3weeks, how
will they know if its is returning to work or
relaxing recreational travel ??? What a mess !!.
13th May we have to tread carefully in the
garden now as three baby blackbirds are
making their first steps and flight around the
back garden. Having no tails hampers their
balance on branches. Mum is busy chasing
and feeding them and still being very friendly.

14th May walked around
'Roberts Field' which must have
been mown as it was covered
in short late cowslips. There
were few butterflies but we
spotted our first small Heath
Butterfly and some small moths.

small Heath
16mm
21

15th May
After the cold spell it is warming up again so we
walked along the Glen from Kate's Bridge along the
dyke. The sun shone and we were surprised
to see a bank of brambles in full flower. Then
we heard the clookcoo again, but did not see it.

16th May Red Kites continued to circle over our
garden getting increasingly lower and lower
searching for food. We expect to see young soon.

Red Kites

17th May

Bird family life is not all plain sailing in the coampin garden. Over the past few days we have found two drowned fledglings in the bird bath, either starlings or our very own blackbirds. John put more stones and a brick for the unsteady to land, in the bird bath. We are very sad and a bit guilty. There followed a dramatic rescue of a drowning fledgling sparrow in the garage sink. Shortly after John spotted a crow on the Rose arch stealing the collared dove eggs. So now we have lost all hope of collared dove babies unless they start again.

18th May Today bird life looked a little brighter as a goldfinch landed on the nigor feeder and delicately ate his meal. This is an unusual bird in our garden.

goldfinch

20th May
The barley fields are looking rather like silky green velvet as the barley heads mature growing whiskers

21st May We walked along the West Glen in the village but we didn't see any fish. However the fallow field had transformed itself into a carpet of purple flowering grasses and bright yellow flowers

View of Carlby Church from Essendine path

24

20th May
View of The Chestnuts, Rosie's house from the
Essendine path across the fallow meadow.

22nd May
It has been unpleasant walking weather with exceptionally high winds of 45 miles per hour. As a result the May blossom has been scattered across the tracks like confetti. Most of the chestnut candles have also shed their petals leaving most of the trees and hedges pure green. Although the elder and guelder rose are in full flower their creamy white flowers are subdued compared to the blousey white May flower. The farmer has cut his first hay field for his horses, it smells so sweet.

24th May I biked to Braceborough, now the wind has dropped to a pleasant breeze. I thought all the sazzy lime green of the spring trees and hedges had dulled down to a corporation green with small breaks of white dog rose and cow parsley. Three brash poppies have sprung up to brighten up ther roadside.

common
poppies

26

A magnificant huge purple thistle caught my eye and the bee on it was golden with pollen. A larger golden sight was a meadow of shining buttercups, what a rich treat. I would have missed the immature lapwing if it had not called 'pee wit' for its parents.

26th May I really missed the cloud of delicately swaying cow parsley; it had been mown by the council to tidy the verge. In its place was the rather Robust hogweed coming into flower at the side of our road out of Cawley.

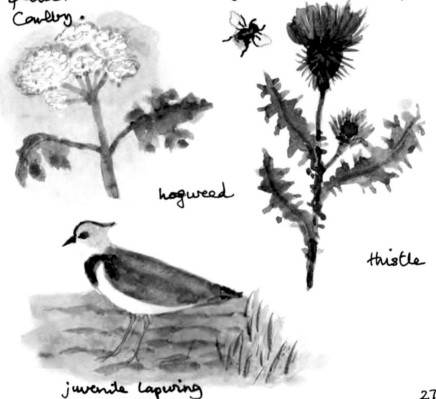

hogweed

thistle

juvenile lapwing

27

27th May

It is my third game of golf since lockdown rules have been eased; the course has been extremely well managed so very few wild flowers dare show their heads. But the numerous grasses are full of flower and swaying in the wind and the yellow flags stand defiantly in the bog garden, which was a pond.
I am starting to see tortoiseshell butterflies in the garden and on my walks.

small
tortoiseshell
butterfly 25mm

yellow flags

28

May 30th
Visited 'Roberts Field' Pickworth to look for
new butterflies and flowers in the designated
meadow. We were not disappointed as we saw
ox eyed daisies, yellow birds nest, cinquefoil and two
common spotted orchids in bud.

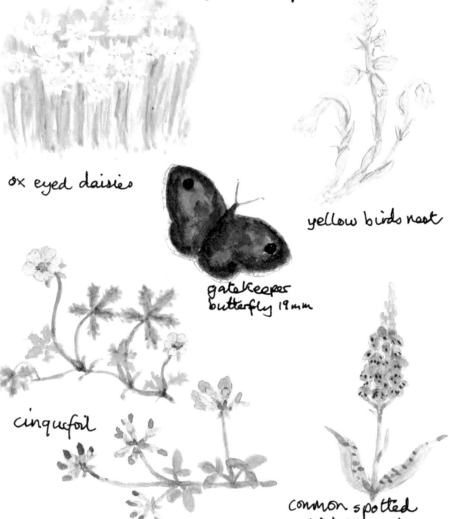

ox eyed daisies

yellow birds nest

gatekeeper
butterfly 19mm

cinquefoil

birds-foot trefoil

common spotted
orchid in bud

31ˢᵗ May

The days of May have been very sunny and hot rising to 27°C but will it last. Both gardens and farmers crop desperately need some rain. We strolled down the Road that had edged grass verges browned, but bright pink mallow fought with bindweed for light. A pair of demoiselle dragonflies fluttered over the West Glen in the sun shine.

lesser
bindweed

demoiselle
dragonfly

common mallow

3rd June The beginning of summer means the sunny days of May have gone and temperatures have dropped by 10°C. Three days of stormy weather has fed the crops. COVID 19 has now caused 40,000 deaths in UK !!!

6th June
The last three days have been stormy with
heavy rain and winds and some really
dramatic skies. The early hot weather and
now the rain means the wheat heads are
fast forming and the barley ears are
yellowing.

storm gathering over Tolethorpe

31

7th June

It was a cool day to sit socially distanced drinking coffee and fizz in Nancy's garden. Against the now familiar gray skies we saw the slow beating of the heron's wings as he flew over her garden in little Casterton. The evening turned sunny and as we strolled down the road we spotted bright yellow hammers in the hedge and bright purple crane's-bill on the verge.

grey heron

crane's-bill

yellowhammers

13th June
As a birthday treat for David we went to Roberts
Field along with Frank and Marilyn!
I had a list from Liz of all the orchids we
should see and we did, I have never seen
the meadow so rich in flowers and
butterflies. It was bottoms up as we made
careful identifications of the different orchids

'Bottoms up' whilst orchid hunting

13th June

Having found two common spotted orchids two weeks ago I was keen to revisit 'Robert's Field' to find more orchids. There were now hundreds of both common spotted and pyramid orchids scattered around the edge of the meadow! I have never seen so many orchids, then we found a large butterfly orchid growing majestically amongst its smaller neighbours. As if this was not enough excitment we discovered several large brownish broomRapes and quite a few dark green fritillary butterflies flitting on the Knapweed

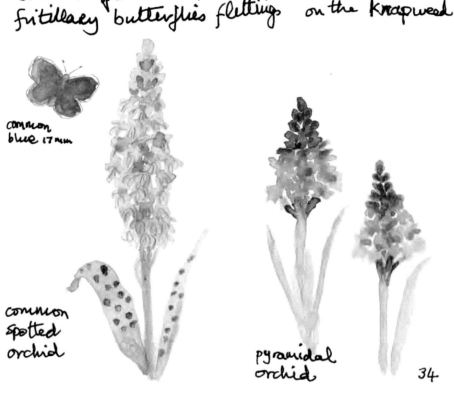

common
blue 17mm

common
spotted
orchid

pyramidal
orchid

13th June
At first we could not identify dark green
fritillary as it was actually a very bright
orange butterfly flitting around the knapweed.
Delicate purple tufted vetch wove itself through the
grasses.

dark
green
fritillary butterfly

knapweed

Butterfly orchid

Broomrape

purple tufted
vetch

13th June
At long last we spot a few swifts playfully flying
over head, what a Relief they have eventually returned

soaring swifts

24th June was
mid summer's day
it was a scorching
30°c!

COMMON ROCKROSE

36

16th June. coffee in Mary and Andrew's garden with giant silver thistles and lakeside views.

24th June

several very hot days were followed by wet
thundery weather bringing much needed rain to
the garden and golf course. The hedgerows are
cream with dusty elderflower and white with an
abundance of bramble blossom, a good year for
blackberries, I think. A large hare streaked across
the golf course, we have seen many this spring
but hardly any rabbits. Where are they?

field scabious   agrimony

38

27th June

The hot weather is over and we are experiencing very strong gusty winds and many sharp heavy and light showers. We walked along the West Glen stream which is now shallow, slow flowing and quite overgrown. Now very few fish are seen from the bridge. The white flowers remaining, like the hedge parsley are tall and delicate and are being replaced by purple, pink, and yellow. The tall teasels are turning from a fresh green to purple where the flowers are opening and the pink willow herb is just opening. The humble common lamb's-tongue plantain looks quite beautiful in flower.

common teasels

Rose-bay willow herb

Lambs tongue plantain

30th June

As we drove to Pickworth some of the grass verges were peppered with bright splashes of yellow and purple flowers. Some of the meadows in Pickworth were also rich in many new wild flowers such as the yellow Ladies bedstraw and the white sweet woodruff and some others still to be identified. As the sun came out so did the butterflies mostly tortoiseshell and some smooth velvety ringlets the spotted female and the plain male.

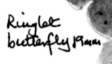

Ringlet butterfly 19mm

lady's bedstraw

chicory

sweet woodruff

3rd July

Just a mile or so from home on a Road we often travel is 'Little Warren Roadside Nature Reserve'. I never realised how Rich in wild flowers it is and I now see it has SSS status, deservedly so. Quite a few flowers on the list we saw in Roberts Field but I was surprised to see on the Roadside. They were Knapweed, greater knapweed, scabious, Rock rose, birds foot trefoil, lady's bedstraw, plantain, broomrape, pyramid orchid, sweet woodruff, hay Rattle, convolvulus, ragwort, larger wild thyme, agrimony, Rest harrow, lesser yellow trefoil, hog weed : Pubs and Restaurants are allowed to open!

great knapweed

Hay Rattle

Rest harrow

lager wild thyme

41

6th July

The first field of barley is being harvested at Essendine, it seems very early. The only flowers in the hedges are the brambles but the verges are edged with pink mallow and purple scabious and knapweed. I was mistaken the barley was ploughed in.

11th July another visit to 'Roberts Field' with Anne and Doreen produced another exciting list of flora and fauna and a few mysteries. The first flower was later identified as a common centaury but the missing butterfly orchid was missing, believed to have been dug up! We saw marble white butterflies which varied in size and pattern, many dark green fritillary and we believed 2 pearl-bordered fritillary butterflies. Later identified as silver-washed fritillary! The cranesbill is everywhere as well as scabions and knapweed and the low self heal. The pyramid orchid has transformed into a strong pink bottle brush shape whilst the common spotted is still evident but nearly over. Tall harebells, a pretty delicate musk mallow and restharrow were new flowers spotted. There were many brown butterflies and six-spot burnet.

Marbled white vary in pattern and size 22-28 mm

42

11th July
More observations from "Robert's Field"

six-spot burnet moth 17mm

common centaury

silver-washed fritillary
35mm

harebell

yarrow

musk Mallow

43

13th July
We enjoyed our first lunch at the
"Six Bells" since lockdown is eased.

Red admiral 30mm

bindweed

small white 25mm   common toadflax

After lunch we walked from witham on the Hill
towards hound. I saw my first Red Admiral and
lots of small whites, bindweed, toadflax and
white yarrow on the roadside.

15th July
COVID 19 has caused 45,000 deaths in the UK.

17th July A large brown dragonfly and a few
butterflies crossed my path on the golf course.
Then a pair of buzzards soared overhead at the
end of my game.

soaring buzzards

brown hawker dragonfly

Sometime after the numbers of deaths were
assessed on different criteria and became 40,000

19th July
We took an early walk towards Witham on the Hill.
The light was beautiful on the ripening wheat
fields and dark dividing hedges. The birds were
still singing and we heard a green woodpecker
yaffle as he flew from a large oak. There was a
poor assortment of flowers growing on the
edge of the fields like common persicaine and
similar creeping plants.

green woodpecker

We enjoyed beautiful tea in a
beautiful garden whilst socially
distancing from Catherine and
Nigel.

scarlet Pimpernel

common persicaria

20th July

John has booked us in to an isolated B and B.
Bowen in Norfolk for 3 nights, what a treat to
escape to another rural location. There is not
a lot of difference between Lincolnshire and
Norfolk but it is flatter and many of the
churches are built in flint. It was noticeably
greener on the grass verges and the farmers
were already harvesting the barley and baling
up the straw and hay in the meadows.

As we arrived early at Hickling we
drove onto to visit Horsey Pump and Horsey
Mere. We shared happy memories of our sailing
holidays we had enjoyed on the Broads, the
old sailing boats were beautiful. We then
walked over the dunes to see the sea and
we were fortunate to see six grey seals
swimming close to the sandy beach.

Horsey Pump

47

21st July

We were relieved, when we emerged through the dunes onto the beach at sea paling, that there were very few people. The dunes were well established with marram grass and a hotch potch of holiday residences sheltered in its lea. Today the wind is a cold north easterly but the sun is strong and the sea fairly warm, for paddling. Again we saw grey seals as we skirted a little tern breeding ground. We watched them fishing and feeding young as well as ringed plovers and waders which may have been sandpipers.

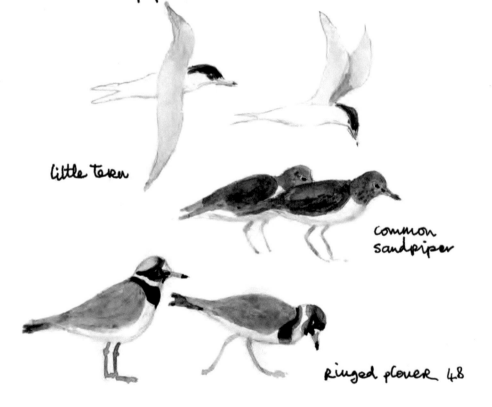

little tern

common sandpiper

ringed plover 48

21st July

In the afternoon we walked from the pretty little wharf at west somerton in the reed beds along the River Thuren and Matham Broad. The broads landscape is very flat, with waving green reed beds and expansive clear skies. Even on windy days, the repetative views of water, sky and reed, I find very calming in these strange times.

marsh marigold

yellow water lilly

white water lilly

49

22nd July
The sun still shines and the light breeze is
cooling, making an ideal day to visit
NORFOLK WILDLIFE TRUST at HICKLING BROAD.
The volunteer warned us that the swallow
tail butterfly comes in May and August, and
that the famous Norfolker Hawker dragonfly
and common cranes could be seen. Unfortunately
we failed to spot them, however we enjoyed
the flora and fauna, much of which is similar
to our local Lincolnshire habitat.

Flower list
blackberry
bindweed
birdsfoot trefoil
bog grass
bullrush
campion
chamomile
dock
fennel
fleabane
hemp agrimony
knapweed
sedge
tansey
thistles
tufted blue vetch
willow herb-great
willow herb Rose Bay
yarrow
water horsetail
branched-bur reed

tansy

fleabane

wild chamomile

22nd July

Although I have illustrated many of the plants we have seen today, in my Lincolnshire diary, there are reeds sedges and grasses too numerous for me to identify. This magical watery broads and fenland landscape is so inaccessible to man but a haven for wildlife. How fortunate we are to have such treasures throughout the UK! The late flight of peacock butterflies were feeding on the hemp agrimony with the odd Red admiral joining in. Such flashes of colour. Then a dash of a stoat into cover.

great
willow herb

stoat

Hemp agrimony
feeding peacock butterfly

51

22nd July
As the many reeds and sedges wave in the wind
you can almost hear them grow for they are
so thick and verdant. All is quiet then suddenly
a coot starts up and a pair of marsh harriers
soar overhead.

common reed   water horsetail   bullrush   meadow
                                                                sweet
                     coot   great fen   52
                                                         sedge

22nd July
Although the hides were closed for health reasons
resulting from the covid virus, we managed to see
a reasonable number of birds. The highlight was
watching a pair of marsh harriers fend off,
a competing pair of harriers, from their prey.
Bird List
Avocet
black-headed gull
Canada goose
coot
egret great
egret little
grebe great crested
grebe little
goldfinch
lapwing
marsh harrier
mute swan
Reed warbler
Shell duck
egyptain goose

little
egret

shelduck

greylag goose

canada
goose

22nd July
It is always a surprise
to see how white the
egrets are. They are
so dignified yet
oriental, too
exotic for Norfolk,
as are the avocets.

great egret

little grebe

great crested grebe

black-headed gull

reed warbler

avocet

54

22ⁿᵈ July

Our bird watching outing has changed into a
dragonfly and damselfly hunt. Today is our
first day to attempt identifying dragonflies, so
there may be some errors. The butterflies have
been magnificant, so many peacocks, small whites
and gatekeepers feeding in the reed beds.

Insect List
Butterflies
gatekeeper
peacock
Red admiral
small white
Dragonflies
brown hawker
common darter
blacktailed skimmer
or
broad-bodied chaser

brown hawker

blacktailed skimmer

common darter

22nd July
As we watched the sailing boats skedding past through
the reeds two pairs of marsh harriers fought over
their prey.

23rd July
Our last day was spent walking more reed beds at Heigham Sound towards the River Thurne. Again we saw clouds of peacock butterflies feeding on the hemp agrimony in the reed beds. As the fen opened up into farm land we followed the pleasure boats cruising down River Thurne before returning to our car. The weather was warm so we returned home with the car hood down.

24th July It is now mandatory for everyone to wear face masks in shops and on public transport, why did it take so long for the Prime minister to see sense? The garden now seems quieter without the blackbirds song, the cooing of the collared dove and pigeon are not quite the same. The chattering sparrows still gather in our front hedge making me realise how much I had enjoyed the songbirds in spring.

2nd August we took an early walk towards Witham on the Hill, the light was so clear. Then a cloud of dust appeared as the farmer harvested the barley. Some fields are already baled and some ploughed up. How early is that! Unfortunately barley yields are down by 30% because of the wet late winter and dry spring.

7th August The walking group explored the country side around Launde Abbey in a sizzling 33°C we heard and saw the green woodpecker and registered that the hedgerows had really turned autumnal.

blackberry

57

8th August
As we walked the Essendine Loop we noticed the
hedges were laden with ripening sloes, reddening
hawthorn berries, glossy purple elderberries
and red gelder Rose berries. Also the Rowan
berries turning bright orange so early, will there
be any left to decorate the church for harvest in
October?

elderberry

sloe

Wild Guelder Rose

Rowan

11th August
It is 33°c and they are combining the barley field
next to our barn, but it is not as dusty as I expected.
Taking advantage of the heat wave they baled
up the straw and gathered it in the next day.
12th August
The searing heat continues to dry up the grass
verges to a golden brown producing seed heads
Reminding us of autumn.

cow parsley   hog weed   thistle   dock

13th August After a week of hot sunny weather a
week of rough stormy windy weather follows. Green
returns to the grass verges and the combining is
interrupted causing more problems for the farmers.
19th August Due to more heavy rain our garden lunch
booked at the Queen's Head had to be moved inside.
However the river Nene looked very green in the
rain reminding me of Millais painting of 'Ophelia.
20th August During coffee in the garden with
Richard and Julia a raucous parliament of
Rooks flew over interrupting our chatter.

59

22ⁿᵈ August

We visited Wicken Fen in Cambridgeshire, a nature reserve which belongs to the National Trust. Due to the covid virus we needed to book the entry to the 'sedge Fen' where we followed a one way system. The Reed and sedge beds were a haven for dragon flies and the woodland for butterflies which were enjoying the late summer flowers and sunshine. A varied habitat was created by Fenland being drained for agriculture by windpumps and then more recently Reversing the process to create more reed beds. Many of the flowers we had seen before and many were now past their prime and turning to dried seed pods. Colour along the paths was from devils-bit scabious, bright yellow fleabane and pale common comfrey with a background of dark purple Reed heads.

devilsbit scabious

common comfrey

22nd August
The oak trees this year have a very heavy crop
of acorns and thrive in this damp location
alongside willow, alder, guelder-
rose, mountain ash and buckthorn.
The most common butterfly as
ever was the small white along
with the peacock, meadow brown,
small heath and a new species
to me brown argus. I was sad to
hear that the swallow tailed
butterfly had not been seen here
for 20 years!

acorns

brown argus 14 cm

side

blue-tailed
damselfly

purple loosestrife

old man's beard

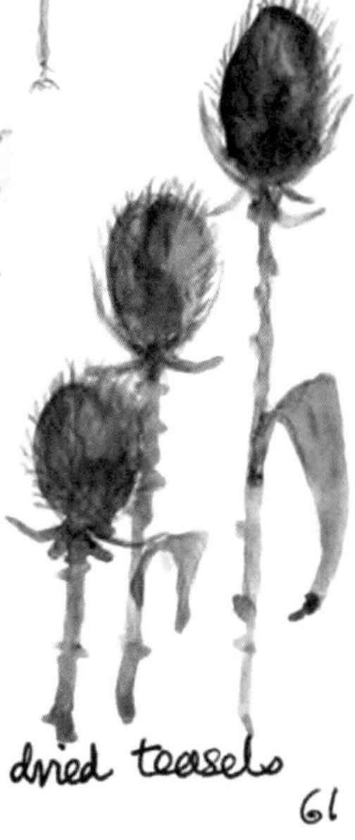

dried teasels

61

22nd August
Wicken Fen is a fantastic location for
dragonflies. We saw broad bodied chaser, common
darter, Emperor dragonfly, Ruddy darter, brown
hawker, common blue damselfly and blue-tailed
damselfly. Our identification of these dragonflies was
assisted by some excellent information boards.

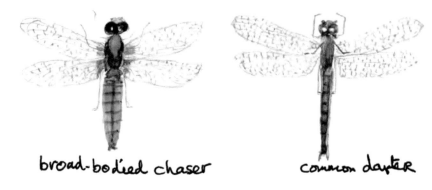

broad-bodied chaser   common darter

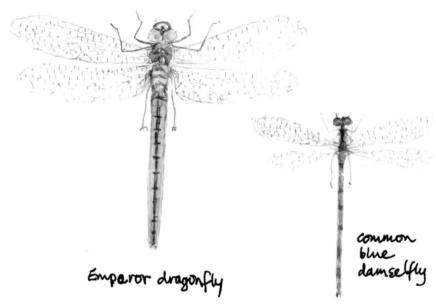

Emperor dragonfly

common
blue
damselfly

62

24th August
Whilst lunching at the Six Bells, socially distancing from Ian and Nancy, we spotted a speckled wood butterfly in the garden. I had seen one before but had failed to identify it in 'Robert's Field'.

26th August
We joined Richard and Julia in a walk in the woodlands of Belvoir Castle. It was a damp rainy day but the slightly overgrown gardens were very pleasant.

speckled wood 21 mm

28th August
I finally got organised to pick blackberries down the road to cook, with the windfalls from Rosie's and Sharon's garden. The wasps were very busy feeding off the ivy flowers near the brambles and the rooks had gathered in the ash tree making raucous chatter.

29th August
We drove to Pickworth and walked into the wood, it was grey and wintery so only white butterflies where out with a little blue chicory and yellow toadflax to add some colour. A kite flew over with missing tail feathers.

Rose hips

hawthorn   63

31st August

We walked towards Witham-on-the-Hill in the bright sunshine and gentle wind. There are not many flowers out now but the rosehips have turned a bright orange and the hawthorn a strong rich red, both shining in the sun. The only butterflies are small whites with one large dragonfly. The fields are rather dull either recently ploughed or poor barley left unharvested and some very black broad beans.

3rd September

Most of the children have now returned to school after almost 6 months of home schooling and holidays. It is far from straightforward for teachers and parents as any cases of the virus, which is having a resurgence, could cause closures. Rosie, David and grandson Elliott came over for a celebratory drinks for our 50th wedding Anniversary. We can have no party but we intend to keep celebrating for as long as it takes!

4th September The warm weather continues. After a good game of golf, Binnie gave us a delicious supper and we all enjoyed her champagne to mark the occasion.

5th September

In the evening we sat around Alan and Suzanne's firepit with more celebratory drinks, we are so lucky to have such good neighbours. A flock of house martins flew over the house and I wondered if they were preparing to depart. I have been recording sightings of swallows and martins to determine the last ones to go.

64

6th September

We drove to Suffolk in the Volvo as it was too cold to have the roof down on my car. We arrived at the RSPB reserve Minsmere ready for coffee and lunch. As the sun shone down I was reminded of the many visits we had made when I first knew John and I was picking up my bird watching skills. Here we were 50 years later still enjoying the fascinating natural world. The reserve is a wonderful mix of coastal zone, lagoons, reedbeds, heathland and mixed deciduous woodland, such diverse habitats. We saw many birds but the flowers were past their best and beginning to dry out and go over.

Flower List
bindweed
chamomile
fleabane
gorse
hempagrimony
ivy flower
mallow
tansy
ragwort
yarrow

crab apple

gorse

Ragwort

ivy flower

65

6th September
Unfortunately the levels of water were very low
in most of the lagoons resulting in a lack of
mud for the waders. In the 1970's we used
to see large quantities of waders; the many
avocets being the star of the show "an orchestra of
avocets"!

Bird List
avocet
barnacle goose
canada geese
common sandpiper
crow
dartford warbler
dunlin
heron grey
lapwing
magpie
ringed plover
shell duck
shovler
stonechat
swan mute
willow warbler
Redshank
curlew sandpiper

barnacle goose

shoveler

curlew sandpiper

dunlin

6th September
Minsmere Reserve was the first place where I
started birdwatching and it is the most important
reserve in Suffolk.

willow warbler

Redshank

stonechat

dartford warbler

magpie

carrion
crow

67

7th September. Our Golden Wedding Anniversary!
Our first night was spent in a huge converted
stables, room enough for many horses and stable
hands. It was also home to many Rabbits enough
for the tale 'watership Down'. In south Lincolnshire
we now see very few Rabbits with haves, once rare
being more abundant.
Before driving to our special hotel we took a
walk along an old railway track besides the
River Blyth to Walberswick. The tide was out
so the large expanse of mud attracted lots
of good wading birds.   swallows on a wire.

Bird List
cormorant
curlew
dunlin
godwit black tailed
gull blackhead
gull greater black
        backed
lapwing
oystercatcher

curlew

black tailed
godwit

cormorant

oystercatcher

7th September

We arrived at the Ickworth Hotel in time for our virtual zoom party with our family in the Middle East. Little did we know that we would see all our family sending us greetings on a "round the world" video created by Jonathan and Tom. They had also created an amazing history of our 50 years of marriage on a video. We watched this enjoying champagne courtesy of the hotel surrounded by chocolates and a huge bunch of beautiful white flowers. We felt very special in a very private way, there were 13 people, us, our sons, wives and grandchildren. Strangely our wedding was also a small affair with 13 people, we are not **superstitious**.

Ickworth an Italianate Palace, Suffolk

69

8th September
We enjoyed a gracious two days walking,
swimming, cycling, reading and relaxing in
the beautiful estate of Ickworth. The herbaceous
borders still had lots of colour and the mature
trees in the parkland looked magnificant. There
are not many wild flowers out but we saw a
charm of goldfinches, a pair of buzzards and a
parliment of very noisey Rooks.

11th September Home again and
the weather continues to be warm
and sunny so it is pleasant to
go to next doors garden for Stuart's
birthday tea. His grandson, Evan.
has baked him a chocolate birthday
cake with a train on the top. We catch a
glimpse of the sparrowhawk hunting the sparrows
who gather in large numbers in our front
hawthorn hedge. In the evening as I pull the
curtains I see some bats flying over the lawn.
A few house martins and swallows
are still flying over the garden.
and the Robin has started singing
again. Suzanne and family gave us a
golden buddhia for our 50th anniversary.

buzzard

Robin

bat

golden
buddhia

70

14th September

We are enjoying another warm sunny week, however there is bad news about the covid virus which is getting worse but not as bad as in May. There is now a big push to get people tested and to join the track and trace app. However because demand is so great the number of tests available is inadequate.

New rules are now in place limiting gatherings of no more than 6 people in home or garden, its bad news for big families. It is no problem to us as both sons and families are locked out in Oman and Abu Dhabi.

16th September the numbers of new cases are rising to those levels in May of around 4,000 daily but deaths are around 30.

Meanwhile the farmer capitalises on the fine days ploughing and planting his fields. We have not seen any swallows or house martins since 13th September.

17th September   I spot the first sycamore turning

71

18th September

The government is avoiding a complete lock down as we experienced on March 23rd but there are local lockdowns in big cities like Liverpool, Manchester and Leicester.

Meanwhile nature follows its normal routine with many trees like the maple and sycamore turning yellow, orange red and maroon on exposed areas of foliage. The poor horsechestnut brown spot disease is proliferating fast leaving some trees looking dried up with conkers dropping fast. The rain and warm weather has encouraged garden and wild flowers to come again. The white nettle edges many paths and roads locally.

white dead-nettle

conker

horse chestnut

I baked a spiced orange cake and it was warm enough to sit in the garden with Sandy and Lee. Unfortunately I had not realised Sandy was gluten free, the rest of us enjoyed tea!

72

19th September
We continue our anniversary celebrations with a champagne tea at Rosie and David's. Once again the sun shone down on us as we relaxed in the one sheltered spot in their garden. They gave us a golden leaved caryopteris which we were delighted with especially as we were given a silvered leaved one, which still survives, from our silver wedding.

21st September
Sue and Carl came around to our garden for tea and champagne, how long can the sunny days and fizz carry on? A few house Martins flew over the garden, these must be the last ones to migrate.

caryopteris worcester gold

22nd September This was the last hot sunny day before the Rains came. I visited "Robert's field" with Doreen and we were surprised how it had lost all its flowers in mowing and sheep grazing. It had reverted to rough pasture until next spring but the hedges held plenty of fruits.

hazel nut

73

22nd September
As well as hawthorn, Rosehips and blackberries
We saw two types of spindle berry wild dogwood
berry, privet and hazel nuts in "Robert's Field"

dogwood

spindle berry

spindle berry

dried knapweed

Today is the autumn equinoxes, equal day and night.
There were 4.000 new cases of covid and the Prime
Minister is threatening new restrictions. However it
was 6 months ago that the first lockdown began.

74

26th september
After four days of wet and very windy weather
we drove down the Road to take a more sheltered
walk along the Ryhall Heath Road. Many of the
small crab apples had fallen on the Road and the
wild cherry leaves were turning a deep rich red.
Everything else was still quite green and bracken
was very lush and the black privet berries
shone richly contrasting the bright red black
bryony berries.

privet

bracken

27th september we walked down to the river
Glen which has got very overgrown with reeds
rushes and branched bur-reed. Water level was low.

branched bur-reed

black
bryony

75

28th September
Just up the road near Witham on the Hill we
discovered a small reserve run by Lincolnshire
Wild Life Trust, called Pitsford. It is a pretty
location on a former gravel workings and
the highlight of my visit was spotting a bright
little copper butterfly
amongst the flowers.
I saw common centaury,
autumn hawkbit, yellow
wort and blue fleabane.
The correct name is Stanton's Pit.

small copper 14mm

30th September - The quinces that remain on our tree
after the heavy storms have turned into beautiful
golden fruit. I picked a few to make quince
jelly and quince gin. The weather is so wet
and windy I want to be indoors.
2nd November A very wet windy
game of golf was brightened up
by the beautiful pink purple and   quince
oranges on the turning sycamores and a
colourful bank of planted wild flowers, at least
eight sorts, some marigolds, cornflower, and yellow
poppies.
3rd October was recorded as the wettest day since
records began. 42,314 people have died from
covid and new cases are rising everyday to around
70, in the U.K.
It is estimated that 1 million people have now
died from covid in the world.   76

7th October we met up with my brother for the first time since the pandemic struck. There were no kisses or hugs as we socially distanced but the sun shone again allowing us to enjoy a pleasant picnic at Waddesdon Manor Park. We did not go into the beautiful French styled chateau but we enjoyed the aviary and gardens. Most of the trees were predominantly green and the cedars were majestic. However the sycamores were red orange and yellow and the acers were a very bright red with the field maple being a pretty yellow. We heard a strange rasping sound in the trees and finally decided it was a Raven as it flew out into the open ground, very unusual for south of England. We were lucky with the weather as it rained all the rest of the week.

Raven

12th October The number of virus cases are increasing rapidly so the government are bringing in more restrictions and different levels in the cities badly effected.

77

14th October

Every evening we hear on the news that infection rates are rising. It was uplifting to watch a T.V. program of Prince William and his family engaging with nature in many different ways. He has endorsed what so many people believe that 'lockdown' has encouraged people to reflect on nature and find solace in it.

As we drove to Belton House we saw 5 or 6 kites, 1 or 2 buzzards soaring and 2 kestrels hovering, all in the space of a few miles. We enjoyed walking among the magnificent trees in the park, the beeches were turning a burnished gold, the maples red, and the diseased avenue of horse chestnuts were bare. The sun shone but grey clouds threaten rain.

Belton House Park

15th October
During a dry spell in the day we took a short
walk towards Essendine. The River Glen was very
overgrown with reeds in some places and there were
no fish to be seen. However the spring flowers are
coming out again maybe because of all the rain
and sunshine. We saw more white dead nettle, pink
clover, white yarrow, yellow fleabane and dandelion.
I think we have seen the last of the small white
butterflies, the last species to be spotted.
18th September It was a cold grey day when we visited
the N.T. Oxburgh Hall. So we were pleased that at
least 4 rooms were open to the public, under
social distancing regulations. Hidden behind
a yew hedge at the side of the recently restored
formal parterre garden, was a colourful old fashiond
herbaceous border. The cultivated bright colours
were a contrast to the unassuming woodland walk

moated Oxburgh Hall

Unfortunately our views were marred by the
scaffolding which eveloped the Hall from the floor
of the moat. This massive project was to renew the roof. 79

19th October
The sun shone as we walked along fields to
Bouton Broad boardwalk. The day before we
had seen some spring wildflowers out again,
but today I was surprised there were many more.
Flower List
Alkanet
autumn hawkbit
black horehound
Chamomile
charlock
common mallow
hawkweed
herb Robert
hemp agrimony
hogweed
Knapweed
smooth sowthistle
white deadnettle
white bladder
campion
red campion
yarrow

charlock

alkanet

black
horehound

autumn
hawkbit 5ocn

smooth sowthistle

1m.
hawkweed 80

19th October
The new constructed boardwalk had been constructed so the public could walk over the very deep muddy margin of the broad to experience the 'carr woodland habitat'. In this watery environment we saw, reed, sedge, reed mace and alder buckthorn forming the 'fen scrub'. As this vegetation breaks down so trees like oak, birch, sycamore and willow colonise. Among the swampy vegetation we saw jays and coots and on the open water great crested grebe and cormorants and black headed gulls. After this pleasant walk we took to the car to visit some more recognised beauty spots on the Broads, enjoying the weak sunshine.

short-eared owl

20th October
We revisited Norfolk wildlife Trust at Hickling Broad as the sun shone but it was too cold for butterflies whilst a few dragonflies were still to be seen. We disturbed a short eared owl which had been resting after its migration.

20th October
After all the wet weather we are very fortunate to have another sunny day in our short break, we knew it would not last. We enjoyed a quiet walk along the nearby beach of See Palling. The bird watching was not exciting with only black headed and black winged gulls. However we saw a few seals of various sizes swimming close up to the shore. I collected a variety of shells, seaweed and feathers.

21st October

On the last day of our short Norfolk holiday it rained all day. We had booked to visit N.T. Felbrigg Hall in north Norfolk which now has a few rooms open to visitors observing social distancing. We enjoyed imagining life in such opulent yet homely rooms with the beautiful furniture and portraits of past family and friends. After we walked in the rolling parkland with a lake and ancient woodland. The autumn colours now show in all the trees accept the oak which still puts on new growth! The huge beeches were now fully turned to burnished gold and the sweet chestnuts were scattered on the ground just waiting to be gathered.

Felbrigg Hall

21st October
Even though we were wet from our walk we
visited the walled garden which had been
transformed into an exotic plant haven backed
by high brick wall for warmth.

Felbrigg Hall walled garden

24th October It is a bright autumn day and the
road to Oundle is edged with bright yellow foliage.

ash   dogwood   oak field   cowparsley
with keys   maple
           The glow of autumn

28th October

As we are still able to be a group of 6, outside, we took a walk around Belvoir Castle with Ian, Nancy, Marilyn and Frank. It was sunny but the wind was cold as we started off from Woolsthorpe by Belvoir following first a river then the Grantham canal. We then rose uphill until we reached parkland with beautiful golden beech trees and a fantastic view of Belvoir castle. We did not see many birds, but a family of swans on the canal and a red kite hunting low over a ploughed field. I saw flowers I had seen a week ago. the smooth sowthistle, hawkweed, autumn hawksbit, bull rushes and common reeds.

hedge woundwort

Belvoir castle

31st October
Another very windy day so we took a short walk out of the village taking some shelter from the hedges. On the grass verges the flowers were still thinking it was spring with chamomile, yarrow, scabious, knapweed hogweed and poppies all flowering. This year we had no children calling on us for Halloween treats, I expect fear of passing on the virus kept people at home.

1st November I saw a Red admiral in Michael's garden. The sun eventually came out between showers and by the afternoon we had gale force winds. We visited Johns brother in the morning socially distancing in their garden, and then on to visit Houghton Hall. Anish Kapoor was exhibiting large stone sculptures and a series of concave discs which created interesting optical illusions inside the house and in the gardens. It was such a beautiful setting enhanced by sunshine and swirling golden leaves of autumn.

Sky Mirror 2018
Anish Kapoor

2nd November

It is another warm sunny day and I played golf
in a team which won, the first this year!
After lunch at the 6 Bells we drove to the
small reserve of Stanton's Pit, run by Lincolnshire
wildlife Trust. I wanted to identify flowers I
had seen on, 28th September, that had puzzled
me. Most of these plants are now growing much
shorter because of autumn conditions being
much colder than spring, their usual flowering time.
Now I identified common centaury, autumn
hawkbit, yellow wort, daisy, blue fleabane and goose.
The willows surrounding the lake were a cool
grey green and this was contrasted by the still
bright red rosehips.

flock of fieldfares

2nd November

At this time of the year I find myself searching
for new flowers so I am recording some that
I maybe overlooked earlier in the year when
my attention was drawn to prettier flowers.
What is remarkable is that those mundane flowers
continue late into autumn as it has been so
warm and wet.
We drove from the reserve to Creeton Quarry which
was a massive but a hidden scar on the
landscape. John wanted to buy some more stone
to sculpt but it was not suitable. However on the
way home we drove through a massive flock of
fieldfares. I think they had just arrived from the
continent and my friend spotted them an hour
later 10 miles south at Tollbar. Their arrival
signifies the beginning of winter, but it is still too
warm for that.

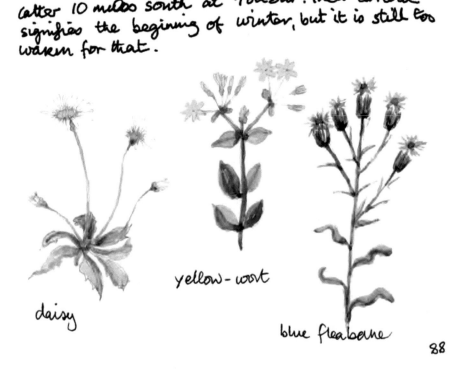

daisy

yellow-wort

blue fleabane

5th November

England has been put into FULL LOCKDOWN again for 4 weeks to try to contain the rise in virus cases. All non essential shops, bars, pubs, restaurants, gyms, golf clubs are to close and travel should be limited to essential business. No socialising in homes or gardens but you can exercise with one person outside your family. We are still allowed caring visits to mother-in-law. Rosie and I cycled to Braceborough determined to keep fit and active. It was a warm pleasant day but the wind came up against us on the way home. There were still quite a few wild flowers on the road side. These were poppies, ragwort, hogweed, mugwort and a bright blue flower with hairy stem and leaf that could be borage of lesser bugloss.

Rosie and I, socially distancing, most of the time as we brushed up our cycling skills. No fireworks tonight. Maybe some on Saturday.

6th November

We took a walk along Dan's track ands as we neared the wood I smelt the characteristic smell of autumn, damp leaf mould and fungus reminding me of my childhood walks in the New Forest. Many of the haws had been eaten but there were lots of rosehips, now quite blue sloes with acorns and crabapples on the ground. Nature has produced a bountiful store this year and we saw a few fieldfares feeding.

7th November

It is warm and sunny and I picked some sloes on our walk to Braceborough woods. Many of the trees are bare but the oaks are still quite green. Along one field margin we saw an extraordinary collection of wild or escaped flowers, some that I had not seen before, and had not been there on previous walks. These colourful plants were cultivated flax, butterbur and white and blue mustard.

flax

butterbur

white mustard

8ᵗʰ November

It is ~~remembrance~~ Sunday and the churches have
been closed so we cannot hold our service but
a member from the armed forces laid a poppy
wreath on the new cross on Carlby green.

Later children came to
lay their pebbles painted
with poppies. Thankfully
the ceremony at the
cenotaph attended by the
royal family proceeded
under social distancing rules.

Rev. Jo led a beautiful zoom service with recorded
music which was very uplifting.

Sadly men fell in the war as leaves fall in autumn. 91

9th November

It is still warm for this time of the year, there are still quite a few yellow field maples, green oak leaves and some red bramble leaves. One or two brambles are in blossom but only yarrow is flowering down Dan's track.

bramble leaves

10th November We took a short walk down the road, the fields are damp dark brown flecked with short green sward of winter wheat. All the ash trees are bare but some hang heavy with dark ash key clusters. Down near the river spring flowers are still out. The red dead nettle, shepherd's-purse and butterbur. Later on I made sloe gin from sloes that I had frozen. Good news pfizer have made a vaccine to protect us from the virus.

Red dead-nettle

Shepherd's -purse

11th November

As I drove around the corner at Tolethorpe the beech trees were speckled golden against the blue sky and dark pine trees. All the other trees are bare apart from the bright yellow field maples and some green oaks.

Beeches at Tolethorpe

12th November
It was sunny and warm first thing, so we took early
walks for the next two days along the road down
to the River Glen avoiding the muddy fields
15th November Very windy so we walked down
Dan's track trying to avoid the strong blast. we
saw some fieldfares feeding in the hedges and the
oaks are now turning from ginger to brown.
16th November It was announced that another vaccine
had been made by a firm called Moderna.
17th November As we walked along the River Glen
I thought that there is less to report on
the changing face of nature. The fallow
field with the smooth sowthistle
had gone brown apart from the
odd dandelion. However
everytime I am outside I encounter
a busy bumble bee seeking the
lost flowers. They are hardy insects.

Bumblebee
buff tailed

19th November It rained all day on the 18th so
when we woke to a beautiful pink sunrise
and a bright sunny day we took an early
walk starting with a short drive up the road.
we then walked alongside the Holywell,
mill Farm Roadside nature reserve. We saw
hazel catkins alongside
pretty yellow leaves.

The virus is bad with
500 deaths and 23,000
new cases daily. The
total number of deaths
is now 53,775 in UK.

hazel catkins

94

20th November
I met up with Sue for her birthday and walked along the River Glen at Little Bytham. In this sheltered valley we saw flowers on white dead nettle, common comfrey, autumn hawkbit and alkanet. It is still so mild. I bought Sue a Mahonia shrub which had bright yellow spiked flowers.
During our walk we saw a cat patiently sitting at the base of a tree.

As we got nearer we saw up in the tree a squirrel aggressively grinding its teeth and chattering loudly at its intruder.
21st November For the last week or so as I draw the curtains there has been the most delicate rose pink sunrises in the East. As I draw the curtains in the late afternoon I have seen some stunning sunsets in the west.

21st November
We had a zoom party for Nigel and Catherines
golden wedding anniversary. Thats how we
party these days! Cheers, congratulations!!
22nd November It is a fine
sunny day so we walked
towards Braceborough to
have another look at the
flowers we had trouble
identifying in field margin.
The strange butterbur had
gone over and dried out
to a seed head. The charlock
still flowered along with
the white mustard, and cultivated phacelia
and a plant from the ~~radish family.~~
phacelia tanacetifolia

Radish
family?

23rd November
More good news, a British vaccine has been
developed by Oxford University and Astra Zeneca.
We are still in LOCK DOWN but we are told it
is working even though 600 people are dying
each day. There are only a few countries world
wide that are recording deaths higher than
the UK. It is hard to fathom why this is so, may
be other countries are not so accurate with
their statistics as the UK.
25th November Often we walk down the road
as the fields are very muddy. It is great to hear
the chuck chatter of the feeding fieldfares in
the hedges and trees along the Road.
27th November we need a change in our walks
so we booked a visit to Anglesey Abbey to walk
the winter garden with its bright winter flowers
and bold structural shrubs and trees. We left
the house in bright sunshine and arrived in dense
fog which never lifted.

magpie   nuthatch

97

27th November

I had really been looking forward to seeing the flowering mahonia, viburnum, skimmia and cyclamen under the stark white silver birches. I was disappointed there was no sun but it did add a rusty mysterious feeling to the fog bound walk. I was surprised to see a daffodil in flower and a little nuthatch, chattering magpie and Thrush singing its heart out.

Anglesey Abbey was once a priory, then an Elizabethan manor house. It was restored in the early 20th century by Lord Fairhaven.

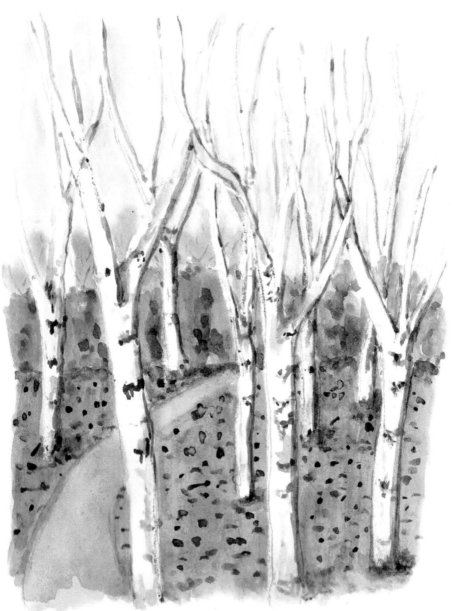

The small intense grove of silver birches is one
of the highlights of the winter walk, Anglesey - 99

27th November
The pink and white cyclamen were very pretty
but I think the best part of the winter
garden at Anglesey Abbey is the structural
plants like the cultivated bramble and dogwoods.

Dogwood and brambles in winter garden

28th November We walked down the road to the
river to avoid the muddy fields. We enjoyed
seeing a flock of chattering fieldfares, a very
noisy flock of rooks which seem more evident in
the winter sky. The flock of starlings did not
quite create a murmuration.
1st December is officially the first day of winter
and it is quite warm.
2nd December is the end of the second lockdown
after a month of closed nonessential shops.
pubs, restaurants and sports venues. Golf restarts.
The terrible figure of 60,000 deaths recorded
in UK with the virus which is unrelenting.   100

4th December
The first snow of winter came today but it was just north of us at Grantham where John had to go to the garage. It was strange to see the odd car driving around covered in snow whilst we only had sleet.

a car from colder climate

5th December
It was sunny but the river Glen was fast flowing and brown and had flooded quite a few nearby fields. Blackberries are still fruiting in mild spots.

River Glen and nearby flooded fields

7th December

This is the first heavy frost -3°c that we have had this year. It has killed all my geraniums and last tomato plant. However the countryside looks beautiful with the hoarfrost decking the trees, plants and grass with beautiful crystal white edging. After only 2 days it warmed up again.

Hemlock decked in ghostly white hoarfrost

15th December
As I drove to the golf course on a bright warm
sunny morning I notice low mist over some
fields. It was especially marked over the new
vineyard at Essendine. A few warm days of 10℃+

A blanket of mist over vineyard.
16th December We went for a sunny walk in
Burghley Park, as it was busy we walked the
perimeter Whilst enjoying a well needed talk
with Nancy and Ian we came very close to a
large herd of fallow deer. They were delightful.

Doe and fawn fallow deer

103

17th December

Matilda, our granddaughter in Abu Dhabi is
6 today. We saw her and her presents on zoom.

19th December As the situation with covid is
rapidly worsening the government are increasing
sanctions. Lincolnshire has for the past few weeks
been placed in tier 3. Restrictions include a ban
on all hospitality venues, visiting other peoples
houses and gardens and many sports, but
fortunately golf is still allowed. A tier 4 has
been introduced to keep people at home and
christmas celebrations have been seriously
scaled down at the last moment; leaving
many families with an excess of turkey whilst
others go hungry and homeless. What a mess!

20th December It is a beautiful sunny morning
so we drove part way to Holywell to pop a
late christmas card into Marey and Andrews.
Holywell Lake looked beautiful edged with a
selection of brown and ginger willow trees.
Unfortunately a new strain of the virus, which is even
more infectious, has been discovered.

Holywell Lake

104

21st December
Is the shortest day in the year and we looked out
for Jupiter and Saturn whose paths were crossing.
This happened and was visible 800 years ago, unfortunately
it was too cloudy for us to see this time around.
22nd December Although it was muddy we walked
towards Braceborough wood, it was warm and
sunny. I was surprised to see the field margin was
still in full flower with yellow charlock, blue
speedwell and white and purple radish family.
23rd December it rained all
day and night heavily.
24th The River Glen burst
it's banks and flooded
Essendine church and farm.
The Nene burst its banks
in Oundle and parts of
Bedfordshire were also flooded. Common speedwell

Essendine Church flooded   105

25th December

The sun shone brightly on the flooded midlands. 2020 christmas proved very different to what people expected or had experienced before. Most families had to scrap their family parties so they could isolate to keep the virus at bay. We did visit Gwen, who is now 101, for just a short time. We spent some time chatting and playing games with our grandchildren, all on zoom.

holly

hazel catkin

ivy

26th December

The cold sunny weather continues but the winter has been mild, hence lots of holly berries and ripe hazel catkins. A sparrowhawk rests after the kill.

sparrowhawk with dead sparrow

27th December

The number of deaths from the covid virus have Risen to 70,000 in the UK. As the situation worsens the country goes into a third lockdown, that is 40% of England is in tier 4 where basically we stay at home except for exercise and essentials activities. So we exercised at Rutland water keeping well off the paths away from other people. Bird watching featured in our walk!
It was another sunny but cold day with night fost.

Bird List

black headed gull
cormorant
goldeneye duck
great crested grebe
mallard
tufted duck
wigeon
mute swan

This year I have been much more observant noting plants that are flowering for a longer season. I have also noted that a sparrowhawk is a frequent visitor to our garden where he preys on the chattering sparrows in our hedge.

male wigeon

female wigeon

27th December
The south east corner, by the dam on Rutland Water
is a popular spot for the sociable, whistling
wigeon and perky tufted ducks.

female tufted duck

male tufted duck

female goldeneye

male goldeneye

male mallard

female mallard

willow

28th December

Since Christmas Lincolnshire has been in tier 4 restrictions so we need to be extra careful and not go into lower level areas like Rutland which is tier 3. We drove a short distance to Deeping Lakes which is owned by Lincolnshire wildlife trust. We drove along side the pretty River Welland where we saw a little egret wearing black stockings and bright yellow "marigold gloves" on its feet! Turning away from the river I spotted a bullet shaped bird flying across an open field, it was a kingfisher, what a surprise, not the usual habitat. As it was cold and icy we took a brisk one way walk around the lake spotting a few good birds on the way.

Bird List
golden eye
Kestrel
Kingfisher
little egret
mallard
thrush
tufted duck
wigeon
wren

Kestrels frequently hover with fan shaped tails when they hunt mammals. We often see them at the roadside with numbers appearing to have risen locally.

28th December
The Deepings Lakes have had a lot of work done to
improve the paths and signage. I read that a
damp area has been successfully cleared for early
flowering orchids, so I must visit in the spring.
It seems strange that we were excited to see a
thrush as we hardly ever do now, yet 20 years
ago they were daily visitors to our garden.

wren

mistle thrush

kingfisher

The numbers of new cases of the virus are now
at 41,000 in a day in the UK. This has risen above
April figures when the pandemic was at its worse
but more people are now being tested. Hospitals
are at breaking point as 71,000 deaths have
now been registered.

30th December

53,000 new cases of covid were recorded yesterday, the figures are shocking and we appear to be doing much worse than any other country apart from USA. No one knows why it is so bad here or if other countries are not so honest with their statistics. However we have HOPE NOW, the Oxford Astra Zeneca vaccine has been approved by the MRHA and will be administered next week. This vaccine is cheaper and easier to use than the pfizer vaccine

31st December The St. Mary's surgery was very busy today so we guess they are beginning to administer the pfizer vaccine. The only New Years Eve party we had was on zoom with 8 friends. Some villages had fireworks at midnight in their gardens.

The last sunset of 2020 over Caulby   garden fireworks

1st January - New Years Day was like no other as the spread of the virus worsens across the world, but nowhere quite as bad as the U.K. and America. We drove a few miles east into the large sky fenland. We walked the perimeter of Willow Tree Fen which is run by Lincolnshire wildlife trust. We never see many birds at this reserve but we didsee some wigeon, a parliament of Rooks, Kestrel and buzzard

111

1st January
At about the halfway
mark we got caught
in a heavy downpour,
luck was on our side as
we sheltered in the only
hide open. No birds to
be seen but this
wonderful rainbow
spread over the flat fen landscape - good fortune for 2021

willow Tree Fen

1st January
After the storm we saw a field of feeding fieldfare
and a skein of pink footed geese. As we drove home a
ghostly barn owl flew along-side the road
hunting the drainage ditches.

barn owl

2nd January
We have booked to visit Belton House Christmas
light display. As it is all outside and it is in
tier 4 we are allowed to go but our friends in Rutland
who are in tier 3 cannot visit it! We think it is
safe to go but the snowfall which settled to about
2" makes it difficult underfoot. It is an inspirational
display but I do not find it as exciting as last
year. As there are lots of flashing coloured lights
it will be difficult to paint, but I will have a go.

3rd January
Theo intended to join the Carlby childrens church
club called "JAM" "Jesus and me" as he did last
month. However Oman was hot and he had a better
offer to go to the beach, but granddaughter Lucy joined.

113

Belton House Christmas outdoor lights

Belton House Christmas outdoor lights

4th January I had my last game of golf with John.
Schools returned after the holidays but I do not
think they should as cases of covid are
steadily rising. There are now 26,000 cases
in UK hospitals and 75,000 deaths have been
reported. In the evening a new 3rd LOCKDOWN was
introduced from tomorrow. Schools to close! 115

5th January
The third LOCKDOWN begins today closing all golf courses, schools, non essential shops, all hospitality and sports facilities. We are so lucky we live in such a big barn and have acres of fields around to exercise in.
As it was muddy we walked down Ryhall Heath Lane and saw the bright yellow gorze against the dense black privet berries. We watched a fieldfare in the hedge flashing its tail, for balance or warning, I am not sure.
6th January we could not believe the news that a mob of people, incited by President Trump, had stormed the capitol in Washington. He will not admit that he has lost the election to Joe Biden.

flashing fieldfare

7th January The temperature was low around 2°C but the sun was so strong it felt quite warm as we walked beside the West Glen river. The light was so bright it highlighted every beautiful detail on the tree bark, tree structure and whole landscape. I wanted to paint everything but could not settle on one thing! So I will paint the church standing against the trees. We glimpsed a little egret nearby.

116

January 9th
Four days of very grey weather and news with
3 million people having had the virus in the UK and
now the death toll stands at 80,000. The good
news is the Queen and Duke of Edinburgh have
been vaccinated today. We can't wait to get ours.
On these grey days I don't seem so observant. We walk
towards Borcebovough, avoiding the mud in the fields.
10th January We walked along Dans track avoiding
the numerous puddles. We passed the horses who
looked so forlorn munching from a pile of hay
in their droopy overcoats that kept the bitter
grey day out.

12th January Its a beautiful sunny day so my
spirits lift after the grey days. It is still very
muddy so we keep our walk on the road and pass
the farmer ploughing his field with a flock of white
gulls picking over the ground behind. As they
fly up they turn from pearly white to grey against
the sun.

15th January

We are experiencing some very wet weather with snow falling on Thursday afternoon. As this melted the River Glen filled up and as the fields were saturated they became flooded in all the low lying areas. Once again Essendine Church suffered flooding from spring water coming up through the floor.

flooded fields near to West Glen river

The River Rose to the top of the bridge and the road flooded. Fortunately none of the village was flooded, as it is all built on higher ground. It was a quiet misty day with only the Rooks shattering the peace and quiet of the countryside.

Good news the snowdrops and aconites are peeping through in the garden and 3,5000 people have been vaccinated against the virus.

aconites

18ᵗʰ January
Unfortunately there are more people in hospital with the virus since the pandemic began. The hospitals are under great pressure and many lack capacity. On average there are 44,000 cases daily and around 1,600 daily deaths. The NHS is doing a fantastic job yet still some people are not taking it seriously.

21ˢᵗ January It is still very wet, the River West Glen is only 18" below the bridge running fast and brown. The nearby fields are still flooded, it is continually rising and falling

22ⁿᵈ January we have had some nights frost leaving some black ice on the road, so Rosie and I decided a walk down to the River would be safer than a cycle ride. We watched the noisy Rooks and the greedy fieldfares in the hedges. I heard swans flying over the garden and was surprised to see only one, it turned its head as if looking for its mate. In the garden the aconites and snowdrops are growing taller and the hellebores are bursting into buds.

a lone mute swan

24th January

We had 4" of beautiful white crisp snow. We challenged our neighbours to a snow ball fight and made a great snowman. You are never too old for a bit of silliness. Two of our grandchildren have never seen snow having only lived in the Middle East. The snow lasted for four days, then the meltwater flooded the fields roads and cascaded down our little River Glea, which burst it banks yet again.

26 January The robin and blackbirds are entertaining us with the most beautiful songs, telling us spring is on its way. However it is difficult to be optimistic when the UK deaths have reached 100,000, the highest in Europe and the 5th highest in the world. Last week had the highest numbers of deaths to the virus but 7,000,000 have been vaccinated. We heard the kites whistling for the first time this year.

29 January
We walked down the road through a minor flood to see the river glen swollen by meltwater. We watched a feeding flock of longtailed tits in trees on the riverside.

Longtailed tits

31st January

It is a year since the first person was treated for COVID 19, it was in Newcastle. A year later we hear that a new variant of the COVID virus called the South African virus has arrived infecting 105 people. Strangely a year ago we were holidaying in South Africa. There is very little chance of us travelling anywhere at present! However we took a walk in Uffington church yard, the carpet of snowdrops between the gravestones was both uplifting and sad.

uffington church yard

3rd February 10 million people have now had the vaccine. Sadly sir Tom Moor died of covid, he had walked a sponsored garden walk raising over £3 million for the NHS; he was 100!
It is warmer so good to do a little gardening, moving snowdrops to a new bed, they grow taller and bigger by the day in the warm sun. As do the aconites. Buds are forming on trees and bushes.
5th February John had his first Astra Zeneca vaccine.

6ᵗʰ February
We drove to Stretton to walk in George Henry Wood, run
by the Woodland Trust. It was difficult walking as it
was really waterlogged. However we saw our first
small flock of Redwings and a charm of goldfinches
flit pass. We heard a green woodpecker and the whistle
of a kite and the turttering of the goldfinches.

charm of goldfinches

feeding flock of Redwing

By chance we met some friends walking there.
We have been having some beautiful sunsets
recently and this evening we had a beauty
from the west and a great rainbow in the east.

6th February   We are enjoying many sunsets now.

Sunset through our sitting Room window

8th February "Storm Darcy" hits the UK but we did not experience stormy conditions but a snow fall of about 4". The temperature has really dropped.

9th February It is cold but the sun is so strong it has melted much of the snow. I had my first Astra Zeneca injection today, what a Relief.

10th A cold sunny day with a fresh fall of snow and another colourful sunset. The next few days are very cold as the snow and ice Remains.

12th February We have a few mornings with stunning pink and golden sunrises, around 6:30 am and I am awake to take a photo. Still very cold.

14th February is Valentines Day, I lead a zoom service for church.

123

14th February.
The snow remains as it is so cold.
St. Stephen's Church, Carlby

sunrise over Carlby with the snow

15th February
Temperatures rose suddenly to 10°C and the snow
had melted during the night. The birds sang
beautifully in the warm sunshine and the melt
revealed the first crocuses and lush green leaves of
wild arum. We saw goldfinches, blue tits, fieldfare and
a pair of Buzzards on our walk down the Road.
We could see how the Leek Glen had risen
about 3" in less than ½ hour due to snow melt.

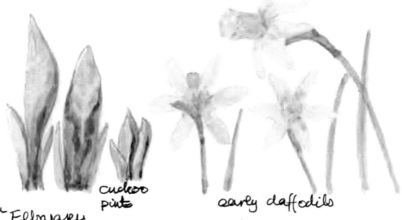

cuckoo
pints   early daffodils

17th February
The virus continues at a terrible pace 12,000 new
cases weekly with around 600 deaths, but this is
a great improvement on Octobers figures! 15 million
people have now been vaccinated which is
very impressive; one of the best in the world.
I spot my first three daffodils in the garden
what joy! Also bright yellow crocuses are forcing
their flower heads through dense growth in garden.
18th February warm but very wet as I walked
with Binnie down the Ryhall Heath Road—snowdrops!

19th February
we, as did two other friends, heard our first skylarks
of the year. They are easy to spot as they fly high
above the fields while singing high chirruping before a
rapid descent to the ground and then silence. The
white nettle and creeping speedwell continue to
flower whilst the broad green leaves of the cuckoo
unfurl under the shelter of the hedgerows. pint
The birds are now full of song staking out their
territories and sharing the joys of spring.

singing in flight

skylark

21st February
Although the little
Egret is quite
common in the UK
now. I am still
surprised to see one
at the side of the
West Glen; they are
so exotic. This one
was in Essendine.

little egret

126

24th February

In Suffolk it is the hottest February day on record, at 18°C; it was quite hot here. This is because of the shift in the jet stream bringing in very warm air from the south. We took a very pleasant stroll down the Road to the river Glen which has returned to normal levels. A bumble bee was collecting nectar from the first crocuses but it was so windy. On our return I searched out the bee finding it hidden from the wind right inside the crocus.

buff tailed
bumble bee gathering
nectar

crocuses

collared dove

I am concerned that only one of our pair of collared doves has returned to view nesting sites.

26th February
It has been very warm for a few days so the waterlogged
fields have dried up so we can walk them again.
Anne and I crossed the footbridge over the West Glen
enjoying the warm spring sun which had brought
out the bumble bees and peacock butterflies. These
are the first butterflies we see as they overwinter
in the UK. The willows looked beautiful in the
strong light and we caught sight of a field vole
scuttling between the gaps in a dry stone wall.

It seems as if these ancient willows besides
the West Glen have become too heavy to support
themselves. Their heavy limbs have broken off.

128

26th February
In the local fields we saw
such treasures.

peacock
butterfly

field vole

27th February to celebrate Johns pending birthday
we had a fondue party on zoom with our son Tom
and his family. It was really good fun; only our mess to
clear up!
1st March
It is St Davids Day and the first day of spring and its
quite warm.
3rd March Johns birthday party is a zoom tea event
with our other son and family who put on a good
show with cakes, hats and games. A more sophisticated
zoom party followed with our grown up friends.
6th March After visiting
the garden centre, one
of the few retailers
open, we walked along
the sheltered river
Tham, Little Bytham.

lesser
celandine

129

6th March
In the sheltered valley of the Tham I saw my first
flowering lesser celandines, white common comfrey,
bright blue alkanet, primroses and late snowdrops.
Everywhere I walk I see lots of male blackbirds and
today a wren caught the bright sunlight amongst
the brambles by the River.

willow   wren

9th March It's a bright sunny day and the
daffodils are bursting into a gaudy display
in the stone built villages that we pass on our way
to Peterborough. Beneath the hedges green sheaths of
cuckoo pint unfurl whilst the pussy willow turns
from grey to fluffy yellow. The days are noticeably
longer. Theo our grandson in Oman is 10 on the 11th March.
12th March Sadly there have now been 125,000 deaths
due to the covid virus in the UK. Meanwhile the
violets flourish in banks by the roadside and on
the bank in Cavlby Church.
                                                    violets
I spot my first blackthorn
blossom in the
hedgerows, it
is late.

130

13th March
We walked across some very waterlogged fields to get to Rickworth wood. We then got soaked by a cloud burst. Primroses looked like treasure in the messy muddy wood and the dogsmercury created a clean carpet under the hazel. Lots of herbaceous plants like cow parsley are shooting up new leaves whilst buds are swelling on the trees and brambles. The blackthorn and Bullace are beginning to blossom.

primRoses

dog's MeRcuRy

budding hawthorn

March hare

14th March Mother's Day in UK. We took an early walk before church in Robert's Field.

14th March
At Robert's Field we saw clumps of purple violets, green flowers of dogs mercury, pussy willow, cuckoo pint unfurling and the hazel catkins were dropping. A pair of buzzards circled above the field.

16th March Binnie and I sat drinking coffee and eating flapjack in the topiary avenue at Clipsham Wood. It was raining but we were allowed to exercise and picnic with one other person now. The blackthorn and bullace are out and tree buds continue to swell on the hawthorn, elderflower, honeysuckle and dogrose. We heard a kite whistling and saw 2 buzzards silently fly into the woods whilst the pheasants strutted about. This year I have notice some variation in colouring, the brown rump being the colchicus group and the grey rump being the torquatus group. I had previously thought the grey rump was an immature bird.

torquatus
pheasant

colchicus
pheasant

St. Patricks Day
17th March It is a great achievement that in the UK 25 million people have now had their 1st vaccine.

132

21ˢᵗ March
walked down the road with John before church and in
the afternoon I walked up Dom's track with Rosie and
around Monks wood. We saw lots of blackbirds, heard the
robins singing, and the yellowhammer 'a little bit of
bread and no cheese'. Some long tailed tits where busy
in shrubs in Rosie's garden. As we are so exposed
the blackthorn has not blossomed but leaves on
elder and hawthorn are coming out. Dogs mercury
flowers in the wood along with pristine primroses
and clumps of purple and white violet. I was
pleased to see coltsfoot in flower for the first time
on the side of the fields.

blue tit

great tit

yellowhammer

coltsfoot

23rd March

It is one year since the first lockdown so it is now a rememberance day for the 126,000 deaths resulting from Covid 19. There was a minutes silence at midday. Numbers of deaths are decreasing to around 112 a day, the good news is half the population have been vaccinated.

24th March I drove to Exton to meet Binnie and we walked to Fort Henry, I have not been there for years. It was very cold but we still lingered for a long chat when we passed Carol who used to belong to the golf club. Everybody is so keen to chat after 3 months of lockdown! We saw a pair of buzzards, kites, yellowhammers, male pheasants, grey partridge and chaffinches in full song. The pussy willow is yellow and powdery and I spot a different sort which is narrow and grey. The "sticky buds" from the horse chestnut are opening up. On the lake we see tufted duck, great crested grebe and a single swan, the other on the nest, maybe.

blackthorn

willow

sticky buds opening on horse chestnut

134

24th March
Today I recognised the song of the chaffinch which was beautiful. I see the house sparrows everyday chit chatting in our hawthorn hedge, they are cheeky little birds. A year ago since first lockdown

house sparrow

chaffinch

26th March
It is very cold and windy so we seek shelter by walking down Dan's track towards Mark's wood. It is so exposed here the blackthorn is only in bud and there are no cowslips to be seen yet. The cold weather has made all the flowers later this year compared to spring 2020 where everything was early.
28 March I do not drive out much as we have had to stay local, not going much further than 6 miles from home for our exercise. I love to see how nature is unfolding and have enjoyed seeing the lambs recently.

British milksheep

Jacob sheep

28th March 2021

A third wave of covid 19 sweeps across Europe; in the UK we hold our breath hoping it will not reach us. Tomorrow the UK's 3rd lock down, which has lasted 3 months, is about to be eased with outside sports like golf and tennis being resumed. Some social activities can recommence, outside 6 people or 2 families can meet up. The vaccine distribution slows with supply problems but it is still one of the best in the world with 95% of all over sixties being done. Problems over vaccine supplies, its efficacy and border controls have become very political. We now have fears that our sons and families may not be able to come back to the UK for their summer holidays. There could be a traffic light system regarding countries that we can visit or people can travel from, and this may keep changing as it did last year.

There is no conclusion to my personal journey in nature study during the covid 19 pandemic, as it still continues. I knew back in February 2020 that the virus that started in China and initially spread to Italy would be significant and need recording. However I never thought it would last so long and that writing and illustrating my nature journal would be so important to my wellbeing. As I continue my observations of the natural environment I realise the importance of its protection and future planning needed regarding climate change.